# THE
# PASSIONATE
# LIFE

## BIBLE STUDY SERIES

# *Mark*

## MIRACLES
### AND
## MERCY

12-WEEK STUDY GUIDE

**BroadStreet**
PUBLISHING

BroadStreet Publishing Group, LLC
Racine, Wisconsin, USA
BroadStreetPublishing.com

**The Passionate Life Bible Study Series**
MARK: MERCY AND MIRACLES

© 2016 BroadStreet Publishing Group

Edited by Jeremy Bouma

ISBN-13: 978-1-4245-5167-5 (softcover)
ISBN-13: 978-1-4245-5252-8 (e-book)

Cover design by Chris Garborg at www.garborgdesign.com
Typesetting by Katherine Lloyd at www.theDESKonline.com

Printed in the United States of America

16 17 18 19 20  5 4 3 2 1

# Contents

# Using This Passionate Life Bible Study

The psalmist declares, "Truth's shining light guides me in my choices and decisions; the revelation of your Word makes my pathway clear" (Psalm 119:105).

This verse forms the foundation of the Passionate Life Bible Study series. Not only do we want to kindle within you a deep, burning passion for God and his Word, but we also want to let the Word's light blaze a bright path before you to help you make truth-filled choices and decisions, while encountering the heart of God along the way.

God longs to have his Word expressed in a way that would unlock the passion of his heart. Inspired by The Passion Translation but usable with any Bible translation, this is a heart-level Bible study, from the passion of God's heart to the passion of your heart. Our goal is to trigger inside you an overwhelming response to the truth of the Bible.

## DISCOVER. EXPLORE. EXPERIENCE. SHARE.

Each of the following lessons is divided into four sections: *Discover the Heart of God*; *Explore the Heart of God*; *Experience the Heart of God*; and *Share the Heart of God*. They are meant to guide your study of the truth of God's Word, while drawing you closer and deeper into his passionate heart for you and your world.

The *Discover* section is designed to help you make observations about the reading. Every lesson opens with the same three questions: What did you notice, perhaps for the first time? What questions do you have? And, what did you learn about the heart of God? There are no right answers here! They are meant to jump-start your journey into God's truth by bringing to the surface your initial impressions about the passage. The other questions help draw your attention to specific points the author wrote and discover the truths God is conveying.

*Explore* takes you deeper into God's Word by inviting you to think more critically and explain what the passage is saying. Often there is some extra information to highlight and clarify certain aspects of the passage, while inviting you to make connections. Don't worry if the answers aren't immediately apparent. Sometimes you may need to dig a little deeper or take a little more time to think. You'll be grateful you did, because you will have tapped into God's revelation-light in greater measure!

*Experience* is meant to help you do just that: experience God's heart for you personally. It will help you live out God's Word by applying it to your unique life situation. Each question in this section is designed to bring the Bible into your world in fresh, exciting, and relevant ways. At the end of this section, you will have a better idea of how to make choices and decisions that please God, while walking through life on clear paths bathed in the light of his revelation!

The final section is *Share*. God's Word isn't meant to be merely studied or memorized; it's meant to be shared with other people—both through living and telling. This section helps you understand how the reading relates to growing closer to others, to enriching your fellowship and relationship with your world. It also helps you listen to the stories of those around you, so you can bridge Jesus' story with their stories.

## SUGGESTIONS FOR INDIVIDUAL STUDY

Reading and studying the Bible is an exciting journey! It's like reading your favorite novel—where the purpose is encountering the heart and mind of the author through its characters and conflict, plot points, and prose.

This study is designed to help you encounter the heart of God and let his Word to you reach deep down into your very soul—all so you can live and enjoy the life he intends for you. And like with any journey, a number of practices will help you along the way:

1.  Begin your lesson time in prayer, asking God to open up his Word to you in new ways, show areas of your heart that need teaching and healing, and correct any area in which you're living contrary to his desires for your life.

2.  Read the opening section to gain an understanding of the major themes of the reading and ideas for each lesson.

3.  Read through the Scripture passage once, underlining or noting in your Bible anything that stands out to you. Reread the passage again, keeping in mind these three questions: What did you notice, perhaps for the first time? What questions do you have? What did you learn about the heart of God?

4.  Write your answers to the questions in this Bible study guide or another notebook. If you do get stuck, first ask God to reveal his Word to you and guide you in his truth. And then, either wait until your small group time or ask your pastor or another respected leader for help.

5.  Use the end of the lesson to focus your time of prayer, thanking and praising God for the truth of his Word, for what he has revealed to you, and for how he has impacted your daily life.

## SUGGESTIONS FOR SMALL GROUP STUDY

The goal of this study is to understand God's Word for you and your community in greater measure, while encountering his heart along the way. A number of practices will also help your group as you journey together:

1.  Group studies usually go better when everyone is prepared to participate. The best way to prepare is to come having read the lesson's Scripture reading beforehand. Following the suggestions in each individual study will enrich your time as a community as well.

2. Before you begin the study, your group should nominate a leader to guide the discussion. While this person should work through the questions beforehand, his or her main job isn't to lecture, but to help move the conversation along by asking the lesson questions and facilitating the discussion.

3. This study is meant to be a community affair where everyone shares. Be sure to listen well, contribute where you feel led, and try not to dominate the conversation.

4. The number one rule for community interaction is: nothing is off-limits! No question is too dumb; no answer is out of bounds. While many questions in this study have "right" answers, most are designed to push you and your friends to explore the passage more deeply and understand what it means for daily living.

5. Finally, be ready for God to reveal himself through the passage being discussed and through the discussion that arises out of the group he's put together. Pray that he would reveal his heart and revelation-light to you all in deeper ways. And be open to being challenged, corrected, and changed.

Again, we pray and trust that this Bible study will kindle in you a burning, passionate desire for God and his heart, while impacting your life for years to come. May it open wide the storehouse of heaven's revelation-light. May it reveal new and greater insights into the mysteries of God and the kingdom-realm life he has for you. And may you encounter the heart of God in more fresh and relevant ways than you ever thought possible!

# Introduction to the Gospel of Mark

In Mark's gospel, we discover a Savior and Servant on the go! What a beautiful description we find of Jesus, the Anointed One. Mark unveils the Lord Jesus before our eyes as the true Servant of God—holy, harmless, and merciful! As God's Servant, we find Jesus very busy in this gospel. At every turn Jesus is active in bringing miraculous healing, release, and love to the world around him.

At an almost cinematic pace, Mark's story of Jesus and his kingdom-realm mission moves forward with great momentum. From miracle to miracle, the reader uncovers a deeper awareness of Jesus' identity and mission until we come to the climax and purpose of his life: the cross. Mark peppers references to Jesus' crucifixion throughout to show his death isn't a tragedy or mistake, but God's plan from the beginning. Through his sacrifice on the cross, Jesus brings in the last days of God's kingdom-realm, marked by miraculous intervention.

We've designed this study to help you journey through Mark's magnificent historical biography of history's most fascinating person, Jesus of Nazareth.

Mark makes it clear that the news about Jesus is wonderful news. For you, and for your world. Mercy triumphs in every page of Mark's gospel, for he writes as one set free from his past and as one who has discovered the divine surprise of mercy. Dive deep into this wonderful news and discover what Jesus has in store for you!

*Lesson 1*

———

# The Wonderful News about Jesus

## MARK 1:1–13

*This is the beginning of the wonderful news about
Jesus the Messiah, the Son of God. (Mark 1:1)*

In Mark's gospel, we discover a Savior and Servant on the go! At every turn, Servant Jesus was active in bringing miraculous healing, release, and love to the world around him. As our Savior, we find Jesus willingly laying down his life for us. Through the cross, Jesus brought us forgiveness for our sins, release from shame and guilt, and victory over death!

We begin our journey through Jesus' story with Mark's appropriate announcement about the *wonderful* news about the Man of Miracles and Mercy. "Wonderful" is a good way to describe it. Here are some more ways: *marvelous, magnificent, superb, glorious, fantastic, terrific, fabulous,* and *awesome.*

As this sensational story of the Son of God unfolds, we find an ancient prophecy of a messenger who would prepare his way. This messenger called people to change their way of living and spoke of the one who would ultimately transform people. Then we get a glimpse into who this one really is.

## Discover the Heart of God

- After reading Mark 1:1–13, what did you notice, perhaps for the first time? What questions do you have? What did you learn about the heart of God?

- According to Isaiah, what was the ministry of John the Immerser? Why was this ministry important?

- Into what did John say Jesus would "bury" people?

- After Jesus was baptized, what happened to him?

## *Explore the Heart of God*

- Mark called the news about Jesus "wonderful." List all the ways this is true and how it unveils the heart of God.

- Why are the words from Isaiah 40 important for Jesus' story? What do they tell us about his coming?

- What picture of God do we receive from Mark 1:10–11? How should this aid our exploration of his heart?

- Mark said Jesus spent forty days in the wilderness. Who else spent a similar time (in number) in the wilderness? Why is it significant that Jesus spent forty days in the uninhabited regions as well?

## Experience the Heart of God

- God used John the Immerser to prepare the way for the people of his day to experience the heart of God in Jesus. If you have a personal relationship with God, who prepared the way for you to have the same experience?

- Mark called the news about Jesus "wonderful." Have you experienced the truth of this in your own life with Christ? How so?

- Mark tells us after Jesus was baptized, the Spirit led him into the uninhabited desert region. There, he endured Satan's testing and encountered wild animals. In what way should knowing that Jesus was tested and tried encourage your own life?

## *Share the Heart of God*

- In what ways can you follow in John's footsteps by preparing the hearts of people you know for the coming of the Lord? How can you help prepare them to share in the heart of God?

- How is the news about Jesus wonderful for the people in your life who need to share in the heart of God?

## CONSIDER THIS

Mark opens his gospel by calling the news about Jesus "wonderful." And it is, isn't it? Spend some time considering and meditating on all the ways you said the news about Jesus is good and wonderful—for you and the whole world. Then praise this wonderful God for his wonderful news that you get to share with others.

## Lesson 2

———

# Come Follow Me!

## MARK 1:14–3:6

*"At last the fulfillment of the age has come!*
*It is time for the realm of God's kingdom to be experienced*
*in its fullness! Turn your lives back to God and put*
*your trust in the hope-filled gospel!"* (Mark 1:15)

Imagine you are a young Jewish man in first-century Galilee. One day a recognized holy man and teacher does something incredible: He says to you, "Come follow me!" This would have been highly unusual, because most teachers, or *rabbis*, as they were called, were sought out by others; they didn't do the seeking. Interested students would seek out such a teacher and ask *him* whether they could follow. Not the other way around.

So imagine their surprise when Simon, Andrew, Jacob,[1] and John were invited to follow *Jesus!* We are invited to do what these men did in response: leave behind our former life and follow him into his new one to experience God's kingdom. When we do, we'll discover what the disciples discovered: the acceptance, healing, and love of the one who came, not to call the religious elite, but everyday people who actually need the hope of a Savior.

———

1  "Jacob" is a literal rendering from the original Greek. This disciple is more widely known as James.

Jesus said the kind of life we've been waiting for has come. It's ready to be enjoyed when we follow him into it. Have you answered his call? Continue reading Jesus' wonderful story and discover why he is who you've been waiting for your whole life!

## Discover the Heart of God

- After reading Mark 1:14–3:6, what did you notice, perhaps for the first time? What questions do you have? What did you learn about the heart of God?

- How did the two sets of brothers react when Jesus said, "Come follow me"?

- Why were the people of the synagogue "awestruck" and "overwhelmed" at Jesus' teaching?

• What reason did Mark give for Jesus forgiving the sins of the paralyzed man?

• How did the religious scholars and Pharisees respond when they saw Jesus dining with "sinners and tax collectors"? How did Jesus respond?

• Why were the Pharisees angry that the disciples plucked grain on the Sabbath? Why were the people watching to see if Jesus would heal the man with the atrophied hand?

## *Explore the Heart of God*

- We learn from Luke 5:10 that the family of Zebedee was in business together with Simon (Peter) and Andrew. They owned a boat and had a hired crew, which makes one think they were somewhat prosperous business owners, for commercial fishermen in the time of Jesus were usually well-off. How does this deepen your understanding of their response to Jesus?

- Mark said Jesus was "deeply moved with tender compassion" to heal the leper. Some Greek manuscripts have "Jesus was moved with anger [at the leprosy, not the man]," though Aramaic manuscripts[2] clearly connote "moved with compassion." The two Aramaic words for *anger* and *compassion* are used almost interchangeably. How do these fuller translations deepen your understanding of 1:40–42 and God's heart toward the broken?

---

2  The Bible as we know it was originally written in Hebrew, Aramaic, and Greek. In recent years, there have been many new discoveries regarding these original manuscripts, especially the Aramaic ones of the New Testament in addition to the Greek. The Aramaic texts are an important added lens through which to view God's original Word to us.

• What do you think Jesus meant when he said that he did not come to call "righteous," but "sinners"? What does this reveal about the heart of God?

• In the context of the religious ritual of fasting, what might Jesus be saying with his illustration about the old and new wineskins?

• Read again how Jesus responded in 2:27–28 to the Pharisees' anger over his disciples' picking grain on the Sabbath. What do you think he meant by his response, and what was the deeper thing he was responding to?

- Why was Jesus' question about whether it is against the Law to do evil or good on Sabbath so important? What was his point, and what does it say about God's heart?

## *Experience the Heart of God*

- What might Jesus be asking you to leave behind to come follow him, like the brothers, in order to experience the heart of God?

- The Greek word for "awestruck and overwhelmed" can also mean "filled with amazement, astonished, panic stricken, something that takes your breath away (being hit with a blow), to be shocked, to expel, to drive out." How have you been "awestruck and over-whelmed" by Jesus' words yourself?

- What kind of religious rituals do we hold onto today that might get in the way of truly worshipping and following Jesus, and fully experiencing God's heart?

- How often do you use the Sabbath as intended, as a day of rest and intimacy with God and family? How does knowing it was a gift made by God for people perhaps change its meaning for you?

## Share the Heart of God

- God longs for us to display the same roof-busting faith as the four men when we bring him our audacious requests on behalf of other people. Follow their example by spending some time in prayer for others in your life who need to experience the heart of God.

- Throughout this reading we see Jesus the Compassionate One on full display, healing and freeing. Who do you know who needs to experience the compassionate heart of God?

- What does it tell you about God's heart for others that Jesus would keep company with sinners? How should we follow Jesus' example in our own lives?

## CONSIDER THIS

Jesus' invitation to Simon, Andrew, and Levi is the same invitation issued to you as well: "Come follow me!" Have you answered his call? Have you responded as these people did, immediately leaving behind your former life and running after Jesus' new one? Spend some time considering this question and how you've responded to it.

# Lesson 3

---

## The Best Storyteller Ever

**MARK 3:7–4:34**

*Jesus used many parables...as he taught the people,*
*and they learned according to their ability to understand.*
*He never spoke to them without using parables. (Mark 4:33–34)*

People love stories because stories connect with the deepest parts of their lives, offering hope along the way. Perhaps that's why Jesus himself used stories to teach. Jesus was a masterful storyteller! At every turn he was teaching deep, spiritual truths through what he called *parables*. These short stories use aspects of everyday life to convey deep revelation-knowledge that people need to hear. He then demonstrated his teachings by rescuing people from hopeless situations.

As we continue Mark's journey through the wonderful story about Jesus, the crowds seem to keep getting bigger and bigger! Yet Jesus didn't shrink and hide. Instead he welcomed them, as he welcomes each of us. As with the crowds in Mark, Jesus shares with us some spiritual stories: one about a farmer who scatters seed, another about a tiny mustard seed that defies expectations.

Listen to what the Best Storyteller Ever can teach you about this abundant life!

## Discover the Heart of God

- After reading Mark 3:7–4:34, what did you notice, perhaps for the first time? What questions do you have? What did you learn about the heart of God?

- What did Jesus do when he gathered his disciples on the mountainside?

- How does Mark say Jesus' own family reacted to him? How did Jesus respond when he was told his mother and brothers were waiting for him?

- Describe the four soils from Jesus' parable and what Jesus said they represent.

- What did Jesus command those who understand his spiritual stories? Why did Jesus say people should diligently seek to understand the meaning behind them?

## Explore the Heart of God

- It is important to remember that in the ancient Hebraic mind-set, to name something was to give it existence, purpose, and function. In the Greek mind-set, it was simply assigning phonetic sounds to an object or a person. When Jesus gave Simon the name "Peter the Rock," he was calling his purpose into existence. How does this deepen your understanding of Mark 3:16?

• Why do you think the religious leaders claimed Jesus was possessed by Satan? How did Jesus respond?

• What is a parable, and why are they important? How do they help people explore the heart of God? Why do you think Jesus used parables so much, as Mark says?

• How do you think it looks to obey Jesus by diligently seeking to understand his teachings? What does Jesus say people who listen with open hearts will receive? What about those who don't listen?

- The Jewish people considered the Torah, God's Word, to be a lamp that gives light to see and understand. Israel was meant to be a light that gives light to the nations. Given this, what does Jesus mean by the parable of the lamp?

## Experience the Heart of God

- How does it make you feel knowing you are Jesus' true family? How should this impact your walk with him?

- Of the four soils in Jesus' spiritual story, which one would you say you are right now? Have you been others at different points in your journey? Explain.

• Consider your listening posture before God and his teachings. Would you say you are listening to God's teachings with an open heart?

• How have you seen the truth of the parable of the growing seed and mustard seed in your own life?

## *Share the Heart of God*

• Why do you think such vast crowds from so far away came to see Jesus? What does this tell us about other people's experience of the heart of God?

- Mark said Jesus called his disciples to his side to experience his heart so he could send them on mission. How should their outward calling inform our own experience of sharing the heart of God?

- How should Jesus' parable of the four soils impact how we share the heart of God with people in our lives?

## CONSIDER THIS

Mark shows us that massive crowds pursued Jesus relentlessly—and he welcomed them! When they did, Jesus taught them spiritual stories about the abundant life he offered and his kingdom-realm. He also extended his physical healing touch wherever he went. Spend time considering what Jesus wants to teach you. And consider what it is you'd like Jesus to do for you—what kind of healing and release you need from him.

*Lesson 4*

___

# The Ultimate Life Helper

**MARK 4:35–6:13**

*"Who is this man who has such authority
that even the wind and waves obey him?"* (Mark 4:41)

What do you do when life shifts unexpectedly? Turn to Jesus! That's what we discover in today's reading and what several people discovered when they encountered Jesus, including the disciples.

One day the disciples and Jesus were traveling across a large sea when a storm reared its ugly head, threatening to capsize their boat and drown them. Not only did they find help in the middle of their "stormy" life shift, they experienced a greater revelation of the person and power of Christ.

The disciples weren't the only ones to encounter and experience our Ultimate Life Helper. On the other side of the sea, Jesus helped a demon-possessed man find release and deliverance. After crossing back across the sea, he encountered a woman subjected to bleeding for twelve years. She had suffered a great deal while under the care of many doctors, but when she met Jesus, she was instantly healed! As if that weren't enough, Jesus also raised a dead little girl back to life, astounding her family and mourners.

At the end of our reading, Jesus sent his disciples out in pairs to do what he sends us to do: to teach and do what he taught and did, to follow his example as the Ultimate Life Helper!

## Discover the Heart of God

- After reading Mark 4:35–6:13, what did you notice, perhaps for the first time? What questions do you have? What did you learn about the heart of God?

- What did the disciples discover about Jesus after he calmed the storm on the Sea of Galilee?

- Why was the man possessed by demons called "Mob"? What did the demons inside the man say to Jesus when he met them? How did people respond when Jesus set the man free from the demons?

- Why did the people from Jesus' hometown take offense at him? Why could he do only a few miracles there?

- What did Jesus tell his disciples when he sent them out two by two?

## Explore the Heart of God

- Why do you think the disciples accused Jesus of not caring if they drowned? What's the deeper meaning of the fearful event on the Sea of Galilee?

- What did Jesus instruct the man who was possessed to do after he left? What might this teach us to do when Jesus does something good for us?

- Compare the two stories about Jairus' daughter and the bleeding woman. In the end, what provided them healing? What can you learn from their stories, especially about experiencing the heart of God?

- It's amazing to see the connection between faith and miracles in 6:5. What does this teach us about God's help in our own lives?

- In 6:12-13, the disciples went forth under the power of Jesus' calling and authority from 6:7. How similar or different was their activity to what we've been seeing from Jesus since the beginning of Mark?

## Experience the Heart of God

- Have you ever felt like Jesus was sleeping on a cushion during your own storm? That he didn't care if you drowned? What was that like? What did you discover about Jesus that helped you more fully experience God's heart?

- Has Jesus ever done something for you that resulted in a loss? What was that like? How did you respond?

- How can Jesus' instructions to his disciples in 6:8–11 also encourage us in our own Christian life?

## Share the Heart of God

- How can stories like Jesus healing the woman and child or delivering the demon-possessed man be an encouragement to those with whom you share the heart of God?

- How might Jesus' rejection in his own hometown encourage us when we try to share the heart of God?

## CONSIDER THIS

Today's reading reminds us that Jesus is the Ultimate Life Helper. He is more than able to handle those times when life takes an unexpected turn for the worst! He is also more than interested in doing something about them—in helping and healing, in releasing and restoring. If life has shifted unexpectedly for you, ask Jesus for help. Then watch him do abundantly more than you could have imagined!

*Lesson 5*

---

## Faith-Lesson Failure

### MARK 6:14–8:21

*"Do you still not see or understand what I say to you?*
*Are your hearts still hard? You have good eyes,*
*yet you still don't see, and you have good ears, yet you*
*still don't hear, neither do you remember."* (Mark 8:17–1)

Consider a time in your life when you were required to have a lot of faith. Now imagine being asked to feed thousands of people with nothing more than some bread and fish—twice! That's what Jesus had in store for his disciples. He told them to feed the crowds with nothing more than a few loaves and fish. And they failed to trust that Jesus could help them do the impossible. Even after they had witnessed Jesus heal so many, save them from drowning by calming a storm, and release people from spiritual strongholds, they still had no faith.

It's no wonder Jesus was so frustrated at times with his followers! Unfortunately, this lack of faith continued throughout their journey with Christ.

Jesus longs for us to trust him. Sometimes he allows us to experience things in order to grow our faith. Continue exploring the fascinating story of Jesus to discover how to avoid the faith-lesson fails of the disciples. Let

Mark show you how to have faith when you need it most and live a life of faithfulness in response.

## Discover the Heart of God

- After reading Mark 6:14–8:21, what did you notice, perhaps for the first time? What questions do you have? What did you learn about the heart of God?

- How did Jesus respond to the massive crowds waiting for him?

- Why were the Pharisees and religious scholars shocked Jesus' disciples didn't wash their hands before eating? Why was this significant to them? In response, what did Jesus say *does* and *doesn't* contaminate people?

- What happened when Jesus multiplied the loaves and fishes?

- What did the Pharisees demand from Jesus when he argued with them? Why didn't he give it to them?

## *Explore the Heart of God*

- How do the disciples respond to Jesus when he asks them to give the crowd food? What does their response say about their understanding of Jesus—and their faith?

- How do you think the episode of Jesus walking on water is connected to the miracle of the loaves? Why did the failure to learn the lesson of the loaves lead to the disciples' reaction in the boat?

- Jesus listed several things that emerge from within people and constantly pollute them. List those things and then write a modern example for each of them.

- What do you think Jesus meant by his response in 7:27 to the woman asking for help for her demon-possessed daughter? Who is Jesus referring to?

- What do you think Jesus was expecting from his disciples when he told them he wanted to feed the crowd? What happened instead?

- When Jesus told the disciples to guard against the "yeast" of the Pharisees, what do you think he meant?

## *Experience the Heart of God*

- Was there ever a time when you felt Jesus ask you to do something extraordinary, as he did when he asked the disciples to feed thousands of people? What was that like? How did you respond? And how did the experience help you experience the heart of God?

- Jesus said the man-made religious rules and laws of the religious teachers nullified God's Word. What kind of man-made rules and laws in our day seem to nullify God's Word?

- Of the things Jesus lists that pollute a person, which do you struggle with the most? What keeps you from experiencing the heart of God?

- It's clear from these stories the disciples still didn't "get it"—Jesus even said as much! Has there ever been a time when God was trying to teach you a lesson and you didn't quite get it? How did that event help you experience the heart of God?

## *Share the Heart of God*

- Wherever Jesus went, crowds flocked to him to find compassionate healing and release. How might it look to live in such a way that others flock to you to experience the heart of God in your life?

- Jesus seemed to suggest that man-made religious rules were standing in the way of people's experiencing the heart of God. What kinds of religious rules in the church might be similarly keeping people you know from experiencing God's heart?

- On two separate occasions, Jesus, concerned about sending the crowds home hungry, ministered very practically to people by feeding them. How can we follow Jesus in sharing God's heart by similarly providing for people's practical needs?

## CONSIDER THIS

Sometimes we can be pretty hard on the disciples. At every turn, it seems they failed to learn crucial lessons of faith and exhibit faith. Yet we often follow in their footsteps. Spend some time considering the lessons Jesus might be trying to teach *you* about living by faith. Then ask the Holy Spirit to strengthen your faith and draw you closer to the heart of God.

## Lesson 6

———

# A Follower of Jesus Defined

**MARK 8:22–9:50**

*"If you truly want to follow me, you should at once
completely disown your own life. And you must be willing
to share my cross and experience it as your own,
as you continually surrender to my ways."* (Mark 8:34)

What does it mean to follow Jesus?

Is it about what you say, by reciting some set of magical words? Is it only about what you know and believe or whether you subscribe to *this* or *that* list of truths? Is it about how you behave, avoiding certain behaviors while embracing others? Do you need to take a class or be initiated?

This is an important question, one that forms the climax to Mark's gospel. As we progress further through the wonderful news about Jesus, the definition becomes clearer—especially as the picture of Jesus himself becomes clearer.

One day Jesus asked his disciples, "Who do people say that I am?" At the time, there were so many expectations about who the Messiah would be. Most of the Jews thought he would be a conquering king. So when Jesus talked about suffering and dying, Peter went a little crazy, rebuking Jesus for saying such a thing!

But, Jesus rebuked him back, accusing Peter of not having his heart in the right place. In this account, he revealed the answer to our question, setting the stage for the rest of this lesson and gospel account: Following Jesus means dying.

## Discover the Heart of God

- After reading Mark 8:22–9:50, what did you notice, perhaps for the first time? What questions do you have? What did you learn about the heart of God?

- What did the disciples say when Jesus asked them who the people said he was? Who did *they*, through Peter, say he was? Once the disciples voiced their realization of Jesus' identity, what did Jesus tell them?

- What did Jesus say people need to do if they truly want to follow him? What did Jesus say would happen when people do this? What about when they don't?

- What were the disciples arguing about on the road to Capernaum? How did Jesus respond?

- Why does Jesus compare our lives to salt? What does he warn and mean by this warning?

## *Explore the Heart of God*

- Why do you think Peter got so angry when Jesus said what would later happen to him? In response, Jesus rebuked him, saying, "Get out of my sight, Satan! For your heart is not set on God's plan, but man's!" (8:33). Why did he say this?

- What did Jesus mean in 8:34 when he taught that if people truly wanted to follow him, they needed to share his cross and experience it as their own?

- What happened to Jesus on the mountain with Peter, Jacob, and John? Why was this significant?

- Jesus responded to the disciples' argument about who was the greatest by saying they needed to receive vulnerable children in his name and that by doing so, they were ultimately receiving God the Father. What did he mean by this?

- Jesus said his followers should let their hand go limp, cut off their foot, or pluck out their eye to keep from sinning. What did Jesus mean by taking such extreme measures? What does it reveal about the heart of God, and how should we follow his teaching?

## Experience the Heart of God

- "Who do you say that I am?" is a question Jesus continues to ask people as they seek to experience his heart. How would you answer the question for yourself?

• How might it look for people nowadays to share Christ's cross? How about you: What are some ways *you* can share the cross of Christ and experience it as your own?

• How might it look today to follow Jesus' teaching about taking extreme measures to resist sinning in order to experience the heart of God?

## Share the Heart of God

• Jesus' question "Who do people say that I am?" is designed to challenge people's assumptions about him. How do people in our world today answer this question? How might it look to challenge people's assumptions about Jesus' identity as you share the heart of God?

- Why is it important to explain to people what Jesus said it means to follow him—to "completely disown your own life...share my cross and experience it as your own" (8:34)—when we share the heart of God?

- Why is it important to our mission of sharing the heart of God that we obey Jesus by being "content to be last and become a servant to all" (9:35)? What happens to our mission if we don't?

## CONSIDER THIS

Anyone who wishes to follow Jesus must die to him or herself and share his cross. It is only in letting our life go for the sake of Christ and his gospel that we will experience true life. Consider how Jesus is calling you to pick up your own cross and follow him. Then commit to dying to yourself to more fully share in God's heart, and passionately follow the Anointed One who died for you!

*Lesson 7*

———

# *Life in God's Kingdom-Realm*

## MARK 10:1–10:52

*"Don't you know that God's kingdom realm exists
for such as these? Listen to the truth I speak:
Whoever does not open their arms to receive
God's kingdom like a teachable child
will never enter it."* (Mark 10:14–15)

At the beginning of Mark's wonderful news story, Jesus declared that the time had come for God's kingdom realm to be experienced in its fullness. He invited people to turn their lives back to God and put their trust in the hope-filled gospel of this kingdom. So we should ask: How does it look and what does it mean to experience it?

In today's lesson, Jesus teaches what it looks like to live in this kingdom by answering a very interesting question about marriage, revealing God's intent for it. He also shares how we enter it, with the humility of a child. The chapter ends with another example of the kind of kingdom-realm life God desires for us all: a restored, put-back-together-again life that mirrors blind Timai ("Bartimaeus"), who regained his sight.[1]

In God's kingdom-realm, things function and are restored to the way he intended them to be at creation. Like marriages, like eyes. We are called to enter and experience this kingdom-realm like a little child, for it exists for such as these.

## Discover the Heart of God

- After reading Mark 10:1–10:52, what did you notice, perhaps for the first time? What questions do you have? What did you learn about the heart of God?

- What was the one thing Jesus said the rich man lacked to gain eternal life? How did the man respond? What was Jesus' response in return?

---

1 The Greek transliteration of the blind man's name is "Bar-Timaeus, son of Timaeus." The word *Bar-Timaeus* actually means "son of Timaeus." So the blind man was named after his father, Timaeus, but we don't know the son's actual name from this. The ancient Aramaic account of the blind man's name is Timai, and Aramaic was a common language spoken among the Hebrews of Jesus' day in Palestine. The Aramaic Timai is likely correct about the blind man's name, especially given the fact that this man cries out to Jesus using an Aramaic title of respect—"Rabbi" (Master-Teacher). In his hour of greatest need and hope, he speaks to Jesus in Aramaic, not Greek, indicating that his primary language was most likely Aramaic, so likely his name was Aramaic too. Now *Timai* means "highly prized (esteemed)." In other words, although Timai was blind, he was clearly highly prized in the eyes of Jesus, who stopped to heal him.

• What did Jesus promise those who've left everything to follow him?

• What favor did Jacob and John ask of Jesus? How did Jesus respond to their request?

• What did Jesus say healed the blind Timai? How did Timai demonstrate this?

## Explore the Heart of God

- What does Jesus' response to the Pharisees' question about divorce tell us about marriage and how God views it?

- When a number of parents brought their children to Jesus, likely in order to receive a blessing from him, the disciples rebuked and scolded them. What does this say about the disciples? What does Jesus' response say about the heart of God and how Jesus viewed children?

- What was the rich man trying to do by asking his question about eternal life and then insisting he'd obeyed the Law since his youth?

• What did Jesus say in response to the disciples' astonishment over how hard it is for the rich to enter God's kingdom-realm?

• What does the favor Jacob and John were asking for reveal about where they were in their spiritual journey? Why did their request defy the heart of God?

• Why do you think the crowd scolded Timai?

## *Experience the Heart of God*

- People nowadays still trust in riches. What other "trusts" stand in the way of people entering God's kingdom-realm? What might you be trusting that's standing in the way of fully experiencing the heart of God?

- Jesus said his followers are to lead by a different model than that of people in power. What are some practical ways to follow Jesus' example of service in order to experience the heart of God?

- What kinds of things do people ask of Jesus nowadays that might not be appropriate, just as Jacob and John did?

- "What do you want me to do for you?" is a question Jesus continues to ask, as he does with Timai. How would you respond? How do you want to experience the heart of God?

## Share the Heart of God

- Jesus' teaching on divorce and marriage is pretty countercultural. How do you think it could help families and couples both inside and outside the church if we shared this aspect of God's heart?

- Have you known anyone who has modeled what Jesus requires of his followers in 10:42–45? How can their example help you share the heart of God?

- Blind Timai represents many in our lives who long for God do something for them. Who can you share the heart of God with, helping them answer Jesus' question "What do you want me to do for you?"

## CONSIDER THIS

Jesus longs for you to experience all that God's kingdom-realm has to offer in all of its fullness. Are you receiving this kingdom like a teachable child or like a rich person who seeks to justify his or her religious activity? Ask God to help you humbly receive his kingdom with open, outstretched hands.

*Lesson 8*

---

# A Different Kind of King Arrives

## MARK 11:1–12:44

*"Bring the victory! We welcome the one coming with*
*the blessings of being sent from the Lord Yahweh!*
*Blessings rest on this kingdom he ushers in right now—*
*the kingdom of our father David! Bring us the victory*
*in the highest realms of heaven!" (Mark 11:9–10)*

During the time of Jesus there were a lot of expectations for the coming Anointed One from God. There were also several people who claimed to be that Messiah before Jesus did. For instance, about 160 years before Jesus, a man named Judas Maccabeus led a successful revolt against the Roman Empire, and many considered him to be the Messiah. As we've mentioned before, the Jews believed the coming Messiah would free the nation from Roman occupation and finally establish the long-awaited kingdom.

Yet this didn't quite happen. God's true Anointed One didn't coming riding in on a white horse; he rode into Jerusalem on a donkey. The Messiah didn't overthrow Rome; he said to pay Caesar his portion of owed taxes.

Eventually, he would bring a different kind of victory than the one the people were expecting: He died to overthrow evil, sin, and death and to bring release and relief from all three.

Jesus was a different kind of King, which demanded a different kind of following, the kind that Israel didn't understand. Jesus summarized what it means to follow him when he summarized the Law with its greatest commandment: love God and love people.

## Discover the Heart of God

- After reading Mark 11:1–12:44, what did you notice, perhaps for the first time? What questions do you have? What did you learn about the heart of God?

- Why does Jesus urge us to boldly believe for what we ask for in prayer?

- What does Jesus say will happen to us if we don't forgive those who have wronged us?

- How did Jesus respond to the religious leader's question about which commandment of God was the greatest?

- Of the people Jesus watched give their offering, who did he say gave the most? Why?

• How did Jesus say his followers should react to persecution?

## Explore the Heart of God

• Why is it significant that Jesus rode into Jerusalem on a donkey? What might the people have been expecting instead if he really was the Messiah?

• When Jesus rode into Jerusalem, the people shouted an Aramaic word that meant "O, save us now (bring the victory)!" The crowds recognized Jesus was Yahweh's Messiah, and they expected him to immediately overthrow the Roman oppression and set the nation free. What does this say about the expectations of the people for Jesus versus what he really came to do?

- The fig tree with leaves but no fruit can be a symbol of Israel's religious system of that day (Jeremiah 8:13; 24:1-10). How does this deepen the meaning of Jesus' actions with the tree? What might be meant by his declaration in 11:14?

- Why did Jesus become so angry with the temple merchants that he drove them out of the temple? What does Jesus' action tell us about the heart of God?

- Jesus used hyperbole when he talked about throwing a mountain into the sea. What did he mean by this teaching?

- What is the meaning of Jesus' spiritual story about the tenants? Who do these people represent?

## Experience the Heart of God

- When Jesus came riding through the gates of Jerusalem, he was received by the crowds with celebration, and shouts of victory and blessing. How have you received Jesus into the gates of your own life?

- Jesus urged us "to boldly believe for whatever you ask for in prayer" (11:24). If we do, he promises we can "move mountains"! What mountains do you need moved in your life? Spend some time boldly bringing your requests before God's throne, believing with great faith you will receive an answer.

- What might Jesus' responses regarding paying taxes mean for our own response to the government you live under?

- Consider Jesus' response in 12:43–44 to the poor widow's offering. Have you thought about tithing in this way before? How should this impact how you yourself give to God, and how you can experience his heart through tithing?

## Share the Heart of God

- What do people in our day often expect Jesus to be? How does he continue to defy those expectations, and how can we show them who he truly is as we share the heart of God?

- Practically speaking, what would it look like in your own life to share the heart of God by following the greatest commandment?

- In 12:38–40, Jesus gave a pretty strong warning about the religious scholars. How might such a warning extend to certain religious people today? How does their attitude get in the way of sharing the heart of God?

## CONSIDER THIS

When King Jesus arrived in Jerusalem, the people shouted "Hosanna," an Aramaic word that means "O, save us now (bring the victory)!" Jesus is ready to bring us the victory in the highest realm of heaven. How would you like Jesus to bring victory in your own life? Bring your requests to Jesus, the King of Kings and Lord of Lords!

## Lesson 9

---

# The End of the World as We Know It

**MARK 13:1–13:37**

*"So I say to you, keep awake and alert—for you have no idea when the master of the house will return."* (Mark 13:35)

For generations, people have been speculating about the end of the world as we know it, probably because we seem to have a general sense that our human story will eventually wind down. But when will it happen? The disciples wondered the same thing. How did Jesus reply?

"No one knows when it will arrive" (13:32), which is why Jesus urged his followers to wait, watch, pray, stand alert, and be awake at all times. This call to stay alert and wait for his return is a call to faithful following and living as his children. Who among us would want to be caught sleeping at his return by living in a way that's unworthy of the gospel we've received and believed?

The world is watching and waiting for the end of the world as we know it. While we don't know when the hour will strike, we can read the signs. May those signs compel us to not only be alert for Jesus' coming, but to also readily share his coming with those we know.

## *Discover the Heart of God*

- After reading Mark 13:1–13:37, what did you notice, perhaps for the first time? What questions do you have? What did you learn about the heart of God?

- How does Jesus describe the significance of his coming and the completion of the age?

- How does Jesus say his followers should react to persecution?

- How does Jesus say people should respond to reports about the coming Messiah?

- Who does Jesus say knows the hour of the completion of the age?

## *Explore the Heart of God*

- Why did Jesus connect salvation to faithfulness and persecution?

- Jesus said in 13:27 that at the completion of the age, he would gather together his followers "from the ends of the earth to the ends of heaven!" What does this say about the diversity of God's family and the heart of God?

- How are the last days comparable to a man who was about to leave on a journey? What did Jesus mean by this spiritual story?

- Why do you think Jesus tells us to "keep awake and alert" (13:35)?

## Experience the Heart of God

- In what ways are Christians hated today for bearing Christ's name? How should such experiences draw us closer to the heart of God?

- How do you think it looks to live always ready for Jesus' appearing? How are you living in light of his second coming?

- How does it look to "be alert" as Jesus urges?

## Share the Heart of God

- Jesus declared that prior to the end of the age, "the hope of the gospel must first be preached to all nations" (13:10). How might Jesus want to use you to share the heart of God and his story with the "nations," even right where you're at?

- Jesus said we should expect to be hated by people because of our allegiance to the cause of Christ. What do these words mean for us as we share the heart of God? How can we take comfort from 13:11?

- How should the reality of the appearing of the Son of Man and the unknown hour of that appearing impact how we share the heart of God with those in our lives?

## CONSIDER THIS

Jesus is right: We have no idea when he will return, whether in the evening, at midday, at dawn, or in the middle of the night. So may we be awake at all times, waiting for his return, watching how we live, and praying that those we know will encounter the heart of God as we have.

# Lesson 10

---

## The Climax of Darkness

### MARK 14:1–72

*"Abba, my Father, all things are possible for you.*
*Please—don't allow me to drink this cup of suffering!*
*Yet what I want is not important, for I only*
*desire to fulfill your plan for me." (Mark 14:36)*

In our reading today, we come to what storytellers call the climax of the story, the so-called *passion narrative* of Christ. It begins with a plot to kill the Man of Miracles and Mercy, a plot one of Jesus' very own disciples helped execute! Jesus' death was anticipated when a woman poured expensive oil over his head and body. It was a common practice among the Jews to prepare a body for burial with fragrant spikenard ointment.

As the story moves forward, it's clear Jesus knew what was coming. He anticipated it when he shared the Jewish Passover meal, offering his disciples the loaf of bread and cup of wine as symbols of his soon-to-be-broken body and shed blood. Later, Jesus was overcome with agony and grief as he stared down what was ahead of him: his arrest and condemnation to death on charges of blasphemy.

While the climax to Christ's story might seem like things had spun out of control, that's the furthest from the truth! Because the one theme that holds this and the next chapter together is that God was unfolding his perfect plan for our rescue through his Suffering Servant, Jesus the Anointed One!

## Discover the Heart of God

- After reading Mark 14:1–72, what did you notice, perhaps for the first time? What questions do you have? What did you learn about the heart of God?

- How did the disciples (compare Matthew 26:8-9) respond to the woman who broke the expensive perfume on Jesus' head? How did Jesus respond?

- How did the disciples respond when the soldiers came for Jesus after Judas betrayed him?

- What was it that finally led the religious leaders to convict Jesus as guilty?

## *Explore the Heart of God*

- The perfume the woman poured on Jesus in Mark 14:3 was made from spikenard (or nard), a spice taken from a plant that grows in Asia near the Himalayas. It was a common practice among the Jews to prepare a body for burial with fragrant ointment. How does this information relate to and anticipate the events that were about to transpire?

- Describe what you know about Passover. How does this historic Jewish holiday relate to Jesus' own story?

- What did Jesus mean when he asked his disciples to receive (eat) his body and drink his blood?

- In 14:22–25 Jesus served his disciples the bread and the cup, meaning he was serving them his death and resurrection, which now is our feast and our constant supply of life. How does this deepen the meaning of Jesus' words during the Passover supper?

• When he prayed to his Father in the garden before his death, Jesus' heart was overwhelmed with "anguish and crushed with grief." What does this say about Jesus' humanity and experience in the garden?

• Amazingly, Jesus resolutely declared that even though he felt as if he were dying, his only desire was for his Father's plan for him to be fulfilled. What does this say about Jesus' mission and his love for us?

## Experience the Heart of God

• The act of devotion by the woman who anointed Jesus with perfume is mentioned in three of the four gospels. You can't read the New Testament without knowing of her passionate act of worship! The gospel will always give birth to hearts filled with passion for Jesus. In what ways can you follow the example of this woman with acts of passionate devotion to Jesus?

• At the Passover meal, Jesus told his disciples to receive his body and drink his blood, which were symbolic of what his body would experience and the blood he would shed. We continue that "meal" with *the Lord's Supper,* or Communion. Knowing what these elements symbolize, how should they impact your experience of the heart of God every time you receive them?

• Has there ever been a time when, like Peter, you denied Jesus or were embarrassed you were associated with him as a Christian? If so, what was that like?

• Just before Jesus was crucified, in anguish and grief he prayed that his Father would take away from him the "cup of suffering." Yet, he quickly added, "Yet what I want is not important, for I only desire to fulfill your plan for me" (14:36). What is your response to what Jesus prayed?

## *Share the Heart of God*

- The New Testament makes it clear that every time Christians celebrate the Lord's Supper, they proclaim the death and resurrection of Jesus (John 6:53-58; 1 Corinthians 11:26). How can this meal be the perfect occasion to share the heart of God?

- While Jesus was in agony in the garden of Gethsemane and prayed he wouldn't have to suffer the cross, he still submitted to his Father's will and willingly went. What does this tell us about God's heart for people, and how can you use this story to share his heart with those you know?

### CONSIDER THIS

Mark began his gospel saying it was wonderful news about Jesus. Now we know why: the Son of God died the death we should have died, in our place! Consider this sacrifice that brought you freedom and forgiveness, rescue and restoration. Spend time thanking Jesus for the punishment he bore during this climax of darkness to give you peace with God.

# Lesson 11

___

# The Man of Miracles and Mercy Sacrificed

## MARK 15:1–41

*"There is no doubt, this man*
*was the Son of God!"* (Mark 15:39)

One could argue the cross was the most horrifying death ever devised. This was how our Man of Miracles and Mercy was sacrificed.

Before a crucifixion, guards would often flog their victims. After this pain and suffering, the condemned were forced to carry their own beam to the site of their execution. Once they reached it, they were laid on the cross naked, stripped of their clothes. Then large nails were pounded through each of their wrists and through both feet—through flesh and veins, tendons and bones.

For hours and even sometimes days, crucified criminals hung totally exposed to the crowd and elements—to flies, birds, animals, and the sun, compounding the excruciating experience. They often defecated on themselves and the ground, adding to their shame. Depending on the time of year, temperatures could reach upwards of a hundred degrees without any relief. Imagine Jesus' struggle, the pain, the suffering—for you, me, the world. And for over three hours!

Through the crucifixion, we see Jesus was both the long-awaited Messiah as well as the Son of God, which, ironically, was confirmed through the climactic confession of a Roman centurion at the foot of Jesus' cross.

## Discover the Heart of God

- After reading Mark 15:1–41, what did you notice, perhaps for the first time? What questions do you have? What did you learn about the heart of God?

- Pilate gave the crowd a choice between releasing Jesus and someone else. Who was that person, and who did the people choose?

- How did the Roman soldiers mock Jesus?

- Explain all that went into Jesus' crucifixion, including the ways he was punished and the events that led to his death.

- Who did the people think Jesus cried out to on the cross? Who did he really cry out to instead?

## Explore the Heart of God

- How did Jesus' death fulfill prophesies from the Old Testament and declarations he himself made during his ministry? See Psalm 22; Isaiah 53; John 3:14; 8:28; and 12:32.

• Why did Pilate ask Jesus if he was the King of the Jews, and why did soldiers later mock him, assuming he'd made such a claim?

• When Jesus was on the cross, he cried out to his Father, "My God, My God, why have you turned your back on me?" (15:34). In what way did God the Father turn his back on God the Son? Why did he do this? Consider 2 Corinthians 5:21.

• Why do think it was it significant that the veil in the temple split in two from top to bottom? As you ponder this, check out Hebrews 9:3 and 10:19-23.

- Compare the reaction of the religious leaders and people to that of the Roman military officer at the foot of Jesus' cross.

## *Experience the Heart of God*

- What does Jesus' death mean to you and your experience of the heart of God? How have you personally responded to it?

- What does it say about the heart of God that his Son would suffer perhaps the most excruciating punishment ever devised—for you and the world?

- How does it make you feel knowing that Jesus was despised and rejected by people, both his disciples and the crowds, to the point of crucifixion? How can this be a source of comfort when people despise and reject you?

- The book of Hebrews says, "We come freely and boldly to where love is enthroned, to receive mercy's kiss and discover the grace we urgently need to strengthen us in our time of weakness" (Hebrews 4:16). The reason why is because the curtain in the Holy of Holies was torn in two—because of Jesus' crucifixion! How should this impact your experience of the heart of God in your daily life?

## Share the Heart of God

- Why is the cross truly wonderful news for the people you know who are far from God?

- If you were to share with someone in your life the heart of God as demonstrated by the crucifixion of Jesus, what would you say?

## CONSIDER THIS

In closing, meditate upon the words of an old hymn of the faith, "The Old Rugged Cross."[1] It best captures the sacrificial death of the Man of Miracles and Mercy. May you yourself cherish and cling to the old rugged cross of Christ!

On a hill far away stood an old rugged cross,
The emblem of suff'ring and shame;
And I love that old cross where the Dearest and Best
For a world of lost sinners was slain.
So I'll cherish the old rugged cross,
Till my trophies at last I lay down;
I will cling to the old rugged cross,
And exchange it someday for a crown.
In that old rugged cross, stained with blood so divine,
A wondrous beauty I see,
For 'twas on that old cross Jesus suffered and died,
To pardon and sanctify me.

---

1   George Bennard, "The Old Rugged Cross," audio recording, 1913.

# Lesson 12

————

## *Hope-Filled New Beginnings*

### MARK 15:42–16:20

*"Don't be afraid. I know that you're here looking
for Jesus of Nazareth, who was crucified.
He isn't here—he has risen victoriously!"* (Mark 16:6)

Hopelessness. Despair. Devastation. Fear.

These emotions must have dominated Jesus' followers at the beginning of today's reading. Who could blame them? In one fell swoop, Jesus' movement of rescue, healing, and release seemed to evaporate. The powers that be had won. Jesus and his disciples had lost. What would that mean for them—for their lives and livelihood?

And yet, like a biting, deep-freeze winter that gives way to a new, hope-filled spring, their hopelessness transformed into relief, their despair into joy, their fear into awestruck wonder. For when three women went to care for the entombed body of their beloved friend, they were greeted by an angel messenger with unbelievable news!

At first, the disciples didn't believe the women's report about Jesus' resurrection, as you can imagine. When Jesus finally revealed himself in full resurrected glory to the remaining Eleven, he corrected them for having such hard, unbelieving hearts. Even so, he then sent them on a mission to "preach openly the wonderful news of the gospel to the entire human race!" (16:15).

Their mission is our mission too. The Man of Miracles and Mercy stands ready to give all who believe salvation, power, and supernatural protection!

## Discover the Heart of God

- After reading Mark 15:42–16:20, what did you notice, perhaps for the first time? What questions do you have? What did you learn about the heart of God?

- What happened to Jesus' body after he was crucified? Who saw it?

- Something unexpected happened when the two Miriams and Salome visited Jesus' tomb. What happened?

• What does Jesus say will happen to those who believe the good news and those who don't?

• What miracle signs will accompany those who believe?

## *Explore the Heart of God*

• To explain away the empty tomb, some people say Jesus wasn't really dead on the cross. How does 15:42-47 refute this claim? (See as well John 19:33-34.)

- What does Jesus' resurrection mean for our sins, even for death itself? Why does it matter that Jesus really is alive?

- Why do you suppose the disciples didn't believe Miriam and the others that it was true Jesus was raised from the dead, even though he prophesied he would be resurrected?

- Why is it important that people believe the testimony from Scripture of those who saw Jesus?

## Experience the Heart of God

- Do you believe the good news? Why or why not? How does believing help you experience the heart of God?

- How have you personally experienced the power of Jesus' life, death, and resurrection?

- In response to the resurrected and ascended Christ, "the apostles went out announcing the good news everywhere" (16:20). How would it look in your own life to respond to the resurrected Christ in this way?

## Share the Heart of God

- The resurrected Christ commissioned his disciples with this charge: "Preach openly the wonderful news of the gospel to the entire human race!" (16:15). Who do you know who needs this news in order to experience the heart of God in his or her own life?

- Before the resurrected Christ ascended into heaven, he said in 16:16 that whoever believed the wonderful news would be saved, and whoever didn't would be condemned. How should his declaration shape how you share the heart of God with people?

## CONSIDER THIS

"Christ has died, Christ is risen, Christ will come again!" should be the hope-filled cry of every believer. It reminds us of the future hope we have in our crucified, resurrected, and ascended Lord and Savior. It also reminds us of the new life that began at the moment of our salvation. Spend time praising God for this hope-filled life, both now and for the future.

# Encounter the Heart of God

The Passion Translation Bible is a new, heart-level translation that expresses God's fiery heart of love to this generation, using Hebrew, Greek, and Aramaic manuscripts and merging the emotion and life-changing truth of God's Word. If you are hungry for God and want to know him on a deeper level, The Passion Translation will help you encounter God's heart and discover what he has for your life.

The Passion Translation box set includes the following eight books:

**Psalms: Poetry on Fire**

**Proverbs: Wisdom from Above**

**Song of Songs: Divine Romance**

**Matthew: Our Loving King**

**John: Eternal Love**

**Luke and Acts: To the Lovers of God**

**Hebrews and James: Faith Works**

**Letters from Heaven: From the Apostle Paul** (Galatians, Ephesians, Philippians, Colossians, I & II Timothy)

Additional titles available include:

**Mark: Miracles and Mercy**
**Romans: Grace and Glory**
**1 & 2 Corinthians: Love and Truth**

thePassionTranslation.com